Shoulder Injuries and Weight Training

REDUCING YOUR RISK

Cynthia L. Humphreys M.S.,D.C.

Copyright 1999 by Robert Kennedy

Published by MuscleMag International
6465 Airport Road
Mississauga, ON
Canada L4V 1E4

Designed by Jackie Kydyk

10 9 8 7 6 5 4 3 2 1 Pbk

Canadian Cataloguing in Publication Data

Humphreys, Cynthia L., 1958
    Shoulder injuries and weight training : reducing
your risk

ISBN 1-55210-013-8

    1. Shoulder--Wounds and injuries--Prevention.
2. Weight training injuries--Prevention.
3. Bodybuilding--Training. I. Title.

GV546.5.H84 1999   646.7'5   C98-900850-9

Distributed in Canada by
CANBOOK Distribution Services
1220 Nicholson Road
Newmarket, ON
L3Y 7V1
800-399-6858

Distributed in the U.S by
BookWorld Services
1933 Whitfield Park Loop
Sarasota, FL 34243
800-444-2524

Printed in Canada

This book is not intended as medical advice, nor is it offered for use in the diagnosis of any health condition or as a substitute for medical treatment and/or counsel. Its purpose is to explore advanced topics on sports nutrition and exercise. All data are for information only. Use of any of the programs within this book is at the sole risk and choice of the reader.

Contents

Sonny Schmidt and Sharon Bruneau

Part 1:
Anatomy of the Shoulder

Ask any serious athlete what hinders progress in the gym and he or she will commonly answer "injuries." To make gains in strength and muscularity, the most important component of your weight-training program is consistency. Sometimes it seems that training-related injuries make this ever-important goal of consistency impossible to attain. For many individuals, the solution is to stop training for a while or at least to avoid working the painful area.

Rich Gaspari

One of the most common complaints among bodybuilders, power lifters and weight-training enthusiasts is shoulder pain. This is not surprising considering the shoulder is the most mobile joint in the body and it is involved in practically every upper-body exercise. A shoulder injury can put a stop to training just about every upper-body muscle group. Whatever you can do to reduce the risk of recurring shoulder injuries will greatly increase your chances of working out on a consistent basis and making consistent gains.

If we consider the biomechanics of any joint in the body, we find that stability is inversely related to mobility. Simply stated, the more movement you can perform at a given joint, the less stable and more injury-prone that joint will be. To understand why the shoulder lacks stability we must look at its anatomical structure.

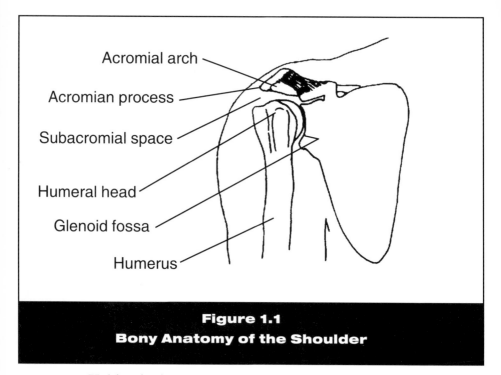

Figure 1.1
Bony Anatomy of the Shoulder

Acromial arch
Acromian process
Subacromial space
Humeral head
Glenoid fossa
Humerus

Unlike the hip joint, which is a ball-and-socket joint and extremely stable, the shoulder could be described as a ball without the socket. It primarily relies on soft tissues including the joint capsule, ligaments and muscles to hold it together. Unfortunately, all of these structures can be overstretched or torn as the result of a single traumatic event (called macrotrauma) or through repetitive overuse (microtrauma). Injury due to macrotrauma is obvious but microtrauma is not so noticeable, especially in the early stage, and we may not be aware that the joint was damaged until later.

It is also important to understand that each of us has a certain amount of joint stability or instability that is genetically determined. This is related to the tightness or laxity of the joint capsule itself and to individual variations in the location of muscle and ligament attachments around the joint. Someone with a lot of flexibility, or who, in layman's terms, might be called "double-jointed" will usually have a higher degree of capsular laxity.

To make gains in strength and muscularity, the most important component of your weight-training program is consistency.

These individuals will have more instability of the shoulder joint to begin with and are typically more prone to injury.

Diagnosing shoulder injuries can be difficult for a couple of reasons. First, the shoulder is capable of performing many different movements and is made of many structures located within a small area. Secondly, shoulder injuries are often the result of more than one interrelated problem. Before you can understand shoulder injuries and the common causes, you must be familiar with how the shoulder is put together. Let's take a look at the anatomy of the shoulder joint.

Bony Anatomy of the Shoulder Joint

Most people think of the shoulder as a ball-and-socket joint. Actually, the "socket" is shaped more like a flat dish. This dish

Michael Francois

is a part of the shoulder blade called the glenoid fossa. The ball is part of the upper arm bone. The bone is known as the humerus, thus the ball is the humeral head. This is illustrated in Figure 1.1. Note that there is no bony support for the shoulder at all.

Anatomy of the Soft Tissues of the Shoulder

The soft tissues around the shoulder are extremely important because they provide primary support and hold the joint together. Several ligaments function passively to hold the humerus and the shoulder blade together. By passively, we mean that they do not contract as a muscle does. Ligaments have some flexibility and elasticity but if overstretched or torn they will not regain their original length, elasticity or strength.

Passive support is also provided by the joint capsule, which is basically a strong and flexible sack that surrounds the entire joint.

Muscles function actively to both stabilize and provide movement around the joint. Active support of the shoulder is provided by four small muscles which reach from the shoulder blade to the front, back and top of the humeral head. These four muscles make up the rotator cuff and hold the humerus in place. Figure 1.2 shows the names and locations of the rotator cuff muscles. They lie underneath the larger and more superficial muscles including the deltoids, pectoralis major and latissimus dorsi. Also note in Figure 1.2 that the tendon of the long head of the biceps runs across the front of the joint and also provides some support.

Figure 1.2
The Rotator Cuff Muscles

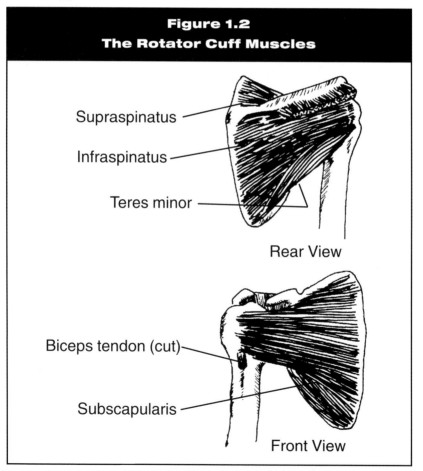

Supraspinatus

Infraspinatus

Teres minor

Rear View

Biceps tendon (cut)

Subscapularis

Front View

The "Roof" of the Shoulder

Another aspect of shoulder anatomy that is integral to understanding shoulder injuries is a structure known as the acromial arch (Figure 1.1). This structure is formed by the upper part of the shoulder blade called the acromian process and a ligament. They both sit above the humeral head like a roof. The space between the "roof" and the humeral head, the subacromial space, contains the tendons of three rotator cuff muscles and a bursal sack.

Lee Priest

The Scapulothoracic Joint

Although not a true joint, another aspect of shoulder function related to shoulder injury is the movement of the shoulder blade over the rib cage. As you already know, the humeral head joins with the glenoid fossa of the shoulder blade. For the shoulder joint to work efficiently, the shoulder blade and the glenoid fossa must be positioned properly. This allows the humeral head to glide smoothly and all the rotator cuff muscles to have the best mechanical advantage.

Muscle Function

When asked which muscles make up the shoulder, most individuals think of the deltoid and upper-trapezius muscles. These are the most obvious and superficial muscles of the shoulder complex.

However, there are several other muscles that contribute to shoulder movement and stability. Next, we consider these lesser-known muscles and their importance in minimizing shoulder injury and dysfunction.

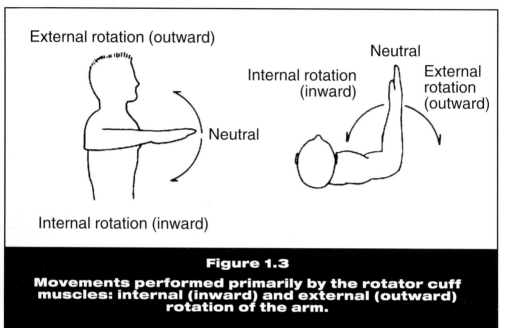

External rotation (outward)

Internal rotation (inward)

Neutral

Internal rotation (inward)

Neutral

External rotation (outward)

Neutral

Figure 1.3
Movements performed primarily by the rotator cuff muscles: internal (inward) and external (outward) rotation of the arm.

The Rotator Cuff

Not only do the rotator cuff muscles stabilize the shoulder, they also assist other muscles in moving the arm, especially in the direction of internal and external rotation. Figure 1.3 illustrates the concept of internal and external rotation of the arm. To get a feel for these movements, do the following:

1. Lift your arm straight out to your side (parallel to the floor like an airplane wing);

2. Bend your elbow to 90 degrees so that your hand is pointing directly toward the ceiling;

3. Keeping your upper arm parallel to the floor, rotate the arm so that your fingers are pointing forward. This movement is internal rotation.

4. Now, rotate your arm back to its original position with the fingers pointing toward the ceiling. This movement is external rotation.

Another way to perform internal and external rotation is to let your arm hang by your side and simply twist it so that your thumb is pointing toward your body (internal rotation). Then twist the arm so that the thumb is pointing away from your body (external rotation).

Two of the rotator cuff muscles, the teres minor and infraspinatus are the main external rotators of the arm. Another rotator cuff muscle, the subscapularis, assists other larger muscles including the pec major and lats to perform internal rotation. The fourth rotator cuff muscle, the supraspinatus, works in conjunction with the middle and anterior deltoids to lift the arm out to the side.

The ability of the rotator cuff muscles to stabilize the shoulder really depends on their strength and endurance capabilities. Another important factor is muscular balance. The strength of the external rotators should be equal to that of the internal rotators. Because the subscapularis has help from the pecs and lats when performing internal rotation, many individuals are weak in external rotation. This suggests that more attention should be given to strengthening the teres minor and infraspinatus.

Strengthening the rotator cuff muscles and developing muscular balance can play a major role in the prevention of shoulder problems and can also help overcome existing problems relating to instability. Some common weight training

Ericca Kern

Strengthening the rotator cuff muscles and developing muscular balance can play a major role in the prevention of shoulder problems.

movements put the arm and shoulder in positions that increase the risk of overstretching or tearing passive structures (the ligaments and joint capsule) that provide support. Strong and well-balanced rotator cuff muscles can partially reduce some of these positional concerns.

Muscles of the Scapulothoracic Joint

We've already discussed the importance of proper placement of the shoulder blade with respect to shoulder function. You can probably guess that the muscles that control and coordinate movements of the shoulder blade must also be strong and balanced if proper placement is to occur.

The primary muscles of the scapulothoracic joint include the serratus anterior, the upper, middle and lower trapezius, the rhomboids, the pec minor and the levator scapula (Figure 1.4). Because shoulder blade movements are complicated to describe, we will not discuss the specific actions of each muscle. It is sufficient to understand that these muscles move the shoulder blade up, down, side to side and generally rotate it in the plane of the rib cage.

Figure 1.4
Muscles that control movement of the shoulder blade.

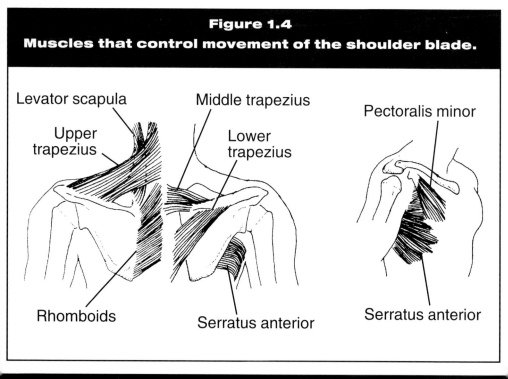

Levator scapula

Upper trapezius

Middle trapezius

Lower trapezius

Pectoralis minor

Rhomboids

Serratus anterior

Serratus anterior

Part 2:
Shoulder Injuries Common in
Weight Training

In Part 1, we developed an understanding of shoulder anatomy and muscular function. Now it's time to explore the common types of shoulder injuries. There are commonly two mechanisms involved in the development of the shoulder injuries seen in weight lifters:
• instability of the shoulder joint; and
• impingement of the rotator cuff and/or biceps tendons.
Let's look at each one separately.

Paul Dillett and
Flex Wheeler

Instability

When we talk about instability of the shoulder, we are actually referring to a condition in which there is a tendency for the humeral head to move beyond its proper position in relationship to the shoulder blade. The degree of instability refers to how far the humeral head moves beyond its proper position. There are several scenarios that may result in instability including:
• genetically determined factors causing laxity of the joint. When this is present it is usually seen in both shoulders;
• macrotrauma or microtrauma causing overstretching or tearing or supportive soft tissue structures;

Debbie Kruck

- weakness and/or muscular imbalance of the rotator cuff muscles; and lastly
- a combination of any of these conditions.

An extreme example of instability is a complete dislocation of the shoulder where there is a total loss of contact between the humeral head and the glenoid fossa. Chances are you know of someone who has dislocated a shoulder. Most commonly, the humeral head drops below and in front of the shoulder blade. A first-time dislocation is usually the result of a sudden traumatic event. It is usually very painful because of muscle spasm. Sometimes there is also damage to the humeral head, shoulder blade, joint capsule and ligaments. The chances of recurring dislocations increase without proper rehabilitation. With subsequent dislocations, supportive structures become more lax, increasing the probability of future dislocation.

A milder degree of instability, resulting in subluxation of the shoulder, occurs when the humeral head is partially displaced. This usually results in a sudden sharp pain as the muscles of the rotator cuff contract forcefully to pull the humeral head back into place. Sometimes this is accompanied by weakness or inability to move the arm for a few minutes. This is termed "dead arm syndrome." Following subluxation, shoulder soreness persists for several days to weeks because of overstretching or tearing muscles and ligaments (a sprain/strain).

Even milder forms of instability can be present that may not be evident initially, but may increase susceptibility to microtrauma through repetitive movements that place the arm in vulnerable positions. This mild form of instability is most common and often contributes to the development of impingement syndrome, which is discussed next.

Impingement

Recall from our discussion of shoulder anatomy that the tendons of the infraspinatus and teres minor are situated in the subacromial space. The space is bounded above by the acromial arch or "roof" of the shoulder and below by the humeral head. The size of the subacromial space varies depending on the position of the arm. In some positions it may become so small that the tendons of the infraspinatus, supraspinatus, long head of the biceps, or the subdeltoid bursa are compressed between the acromial arch and the humeral head. Figure 2.1 depicts the position of the rotator cuff tendons with respect to the acromial arch with the arm in a relaxed position.

Figure 2.1

Position of the rotator cuff tendons with respect to the acromial arch.

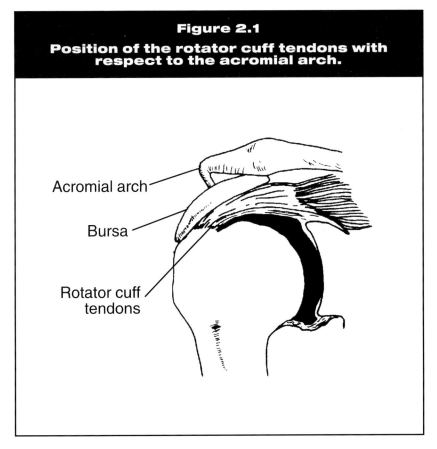

Acromial arch

Bursa

Rotator cuff tendons

Living with chronic shoulder pain is neither necessary nor beneficial.

Some commonly used weight training movements position the arm such that the space is decreased and soft-tissue structures are compressed. Repetitive movements in these positions can result in damage to the rotator cuff and biceps tendons. When this situation occurs, the tendons are said to be impinged. If the activities causing impingement are continued, the tendons often become swollen and inflamed over time and tendonitis results. When inflamed, the tendons actually occupy more of the subacromial space and a self-perpetuating cycle ensues whereby swelling increases impingement and vice-versa. This condition is known as impingement syndrome.

There is much debate over the actual causes of impingement syndrome. Some theories emphasize anatomical or structural factors. For example, in some individuals, the acromian process is "hook-shaped" with the hook pointing down

Flex Wheeler and
Kevin Levrone

Bill Davey

into the subacromial space. These individuals are more prone to experience problems related to impingement. Other structural factors that may contribute to impingement are capsular or ligamentous laxity because lack of passive support allows the humeral head to migrate upward, decreasing the subacromial space.

Other theories exist regarding the causes of impingement syndrome. The most likely scenario is that several different factors acting together contribute to the development of impingement syndrome.

Lee Apperson

Long-Term Effects of Impingement

Many weightlifters are plagued with chronic, recurring shoulder pain and injuries and just "work through" the problems. Others take time off until the pain ceases or decreases and then go back to the same training regimen. Shoulder pain becomes an accepted part of the routine, sometimes for years. Living with chronic shoulder pain is neither necessary nor beneficial. Continuing to perform activities or movements that cause instantaneous or delayed shoulder pain increases your risk of developing long-term problems including early degeneration of the rotator cuff tendons and the shoulder joint (bones or capsule).

Degeneration of the rotator cuff tendons causes a reduction in tendon strength and may eventually lead to a rupture of the tendons. Degeneration of the shoulder joint itself usually leads to a form of arthritis. Typical complaints include deep pain in the joint and associated stiffness.

Part 3:
Overhauling Your Workout to Prevent Shoulder Injury

Now we'll take a look at how you can modify your upper-body training to decrease the risk of developing shoulder problems.

Modifying Common Exercises that Promote Injury

It is important to bear in mind that some individuals are more prone to shoulder problems than others. As discussed previously, some individuals are born with more joint laxity than others. And some of us have certain anatomical or structural features that increase the risk of developing impingement-related problems.

Every weightlifter can decrease his or her chances of shoulder injury fairly easily. Even if you are lucky and seem to be immune (thus far) to shoulder pain, heaving heavy weights around for years will eventually take its toll. Be aware that professional and elite amateur bodybuilders may recommend particular exercises or a particular way to execute a movement and not be aware of the potential dangers involved. Success as a bodybuilder does not make someone an expert in biomechanics or sports injuries. Remember also, elite bodybuilders often use substances that enhance their ability to recover from workouts. Therefore, they may not experience some of the problems encountered by the ordinary individual. It is recommended that everyone include strengthening exercises for the shoulder girdle in his or her training regimen, and omit or modify exercises that can lead to shoulder injury.

The late Andreas Munzer

Modifying Movements that Promote Instability

It seems that many exercises for the chest emphasize getting a maximum stretch of the pec major muscles. This notion that a maximum stretch is necessary to get the most out of a movement couldn't be further from the truth. It's true that putting a muscle into a stretched position allows a fuller range of motion. It also allows you to work the muscle more fully because an inherent

Figure 3.1
Brandy Hale demonstrates the correct execution of dumbell flyes with elbows bent and a moderate stretch of the pecs (top). Elbows straightened and overstretching of the anterior shoulder promotes instability (bottom).

reaction, called the myotatic reflex, causes the stretched muscle to contract with more power. However, what some would consider a maximum stretch, goes far beyond what is necessary to achieve results and may actually cause more harm than good.

Every weight-lifter can decrease his or her chances of shoulder injury fairly easily.

To reduce your chances of developing a shoulder problem because of instability, you must modify movements so that the joint capsule and ligaments are not overstretched. Instability can occur in the front or rear portion of the shoulder, or underneath the shoulder in the area of the armpit. Because many common movements put the shoulder in a position that overstretches the front (or anterior) shoulder, this is the most common area for instability to occur.

The three general rules for modifying movements to prevent instability are:

1. Never use extremely wide hand placements. Approximately one inch greater than shoulder width is suggested.

Figure 3.2
Front military presses reduce overstretching the anterior shoulder (top), while behind-the-neck presses increase the risk of developing instability (bottom).

Figure 3.3
Pulldowns to the chest reduce overstretching the anterior shoulder, (right) while behind-the-neck pulldowns promote anterior instability (bottom).

2. Omit behind-the-neck movements and replace them with front movements.

3. Never overstretch during an exercise. Stop when you feel a slight or comfortable stretch. More specifically, the risk of overstretching the anterior shoulder can be diminished by:

• Using a narrower grip on pressing movements such as bench presses. Place your hands no wider than about one inch greater than shoulder width.

• Avoiding "guillotine" pressing movements that bring the bar to the neck on flat, incline-, and decline-bench presses.

• Bending your arms at the elbow on dumbell flyes, cable crossovers and on the pec-dek, and using reasonable poundages (Figure 3.1). It is most important to stop the movement when you begin to feel a stretch. Going beyond this point will overstretch the front of the shoulder and does not add to the effectiveness of the movement.

- Replacing behind-the-neck military presses with front presses, such that the bar is brought in front of the body rather than behind the head (Figure 3.2). If you feel this will place too much emphasis on the anterior deltoids, make sure you are sitting up straight while pressing. Another option is to substitute overhead dumbell presses for military presses.
- Modifying lat pulldowns such that the bar is brought to the chest rather than behind the head, and also using a closer hand placement (see Figure 3.3).
- Substituting close-grip chin ups (which also greatly strengthens the serratus anterior), front chin ups or underhand chin ups for rear chin ups (Figure 3.4). Also use a narrower grip (hands no more than one inch greater than shoulder width). The notion that a wide grip builds a wider back just isn't true.

Figure 3.4
Close-grip chin ups decrease overstretching of the anterior shoulder and also strengthen the serratus anterior (left). Rear chin ups overstretch the anterior shoulder (right). – Jeff Poulin

Dale Tomita

The rear portion of the shoulder is vulnerable to over-stretching when the arm is loaded in a way that directs the humeral head to the rear as in close-grip presses or when performing push-ups with a narrow hand placement. The risk of overstretching the rear part of the shoulder may be diminished by decreasing the amount of weight used in close-grip pressing exercises. If you feel you will be sacrificing strength or muscularity by using light poundages, perform the movement in slow motion.

To reduce the risk of developing instability underneath the shoulder, modify military pressing by taking a closer grip and substitute front presses for behind-the-neck presses. Be sure to sit up straight to reduce emphasis on the anterior portion of the deltoid (Figure 3.2).

Modifying Movements that Promote Impingement

The impingement position occurs when the arm is lifted away from the body as when performing dumbell lateral or front raises (used to strengthen the deltoids) or with the arm overhead. Impingement is increased even more in these positions by internal rotation of the arm.

The general rule of thumb (literally) for reducing the risk of impingement: When performing a movement that puts the elbow above shoulder height, position the hand so that the thumb is pointing out (the underhand position) or the palms are facing in. This takes the arm out of the maximum impingement position.

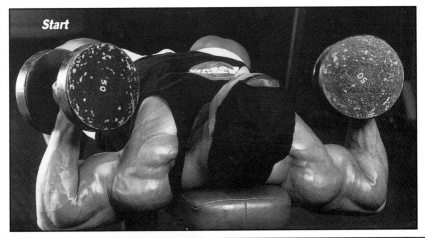

Start

Finish

Figure 3.5
Dumbell presses with palms in decreases the risk of impingement.
– Jeff Poulin

Modifications to common exercises that put the shoulder in the impingement position are as follows:

• Bench presses and military presses may be modified by using dumbells and performing the movement with the palms facing in rather than forward (Figure 3.5). This will externally rotate the arm and decrease impingement.

• Overhead movements such as French presses for triceps (lying or standing), and overhead triceps extensions (dumbell or cable) should also be performed with the palms facing in rather than forward, to decrease internal rotation of the arm.

• Lat pulldowns to the chest can be performed in the underhanded position (which, by the way, puts the lats in their most contracted position and results in a tremendous pump), or with a bar that allows the palms to face in. Similarly, close-grip and underhand chin ups are superior to overhand chins for reducing impingement.

Penny Price

- Avoid the common advice to turn the pinky up when performing lateral dumbell raises, as this internally rotates the arm. Equally important is to avoid raising the elbows higher than the shoulders (Figure 3.6).
- When performing front raises to strengthen the anterior deltoid avoid the palms-down position since this maximizes internal rotation of the arm. Instead perform the movement with palms facing in and don't lift the elbows above shoulder height (Figure 3.7).

Figure 3.6
Brandy Hale correctly executes lateral raises (top). Avoid bringing your elbows above shoulder height and turning your pinkies up (bottom).

Part 4:
Decreasing the Risk of Shoulder Injury

Learning how to efficiently and maximally strengthen the rotator cuff and shoulder blade muscles to further reduce your chances of developing shoulder problems is very important.

Strengthening Exercises to Promote Shoulder Stability and Muscular Balance

The muscles of the rotator cuff are often overlooked in a weight training regimen, as are the muscles that assist in proper positioning of the shoulder blade. To address these muscles you should add five new movements to your training routine. In addition to strengthening the supportive muscles of the shoulder, performing these exercises prior to training your upper body serves as a great shoulder warmup. It is important to remember that the purpose behind these movements is not to build size,

Figure 3.7
Front raises with palms in reduces impingement (left). As normally executed, front raises put the arm in the maximum impingement position (right). – Brandy Hale

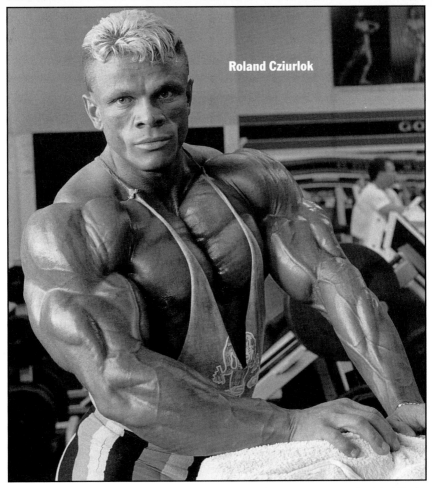

Roland Cziurlok

but to improve muscular balance, strength and endurance. The exercises should be performed slowly and strictly, using resistance that allows you to complete about 20 repetitions. You should work up to performing two or three sets before increasing the amount of resistance.

Some individuals may be resistant to lengthening their workout by adding more exercises. Actually, two of the movements may be inserted into other parts of your upper-body routine as discussed below. The other three exercises will serve to warmup the shoulder girdle, further reducing the chance of injury.

The exercises described here are not those most commonly prescribed to strengthen the rotator cuff muscles. Most often, individuals are advised to perform internal and external rotation with some type of resistance, either dumbells, cables, or elastic tubing (Figure 4.1). These exercises will definitely improve

Figure 4.1
This commonly prescribed exercise for strengthening the external rotators does not provide maximal muscular stimulation. – Jeff Poulin

rotator cuff strength, however, recent research using electromyography shows there are other exercises that provide maximal stimulation of the rotator cuff muscles and prime movers of the shoulder blade. These exercises also have a high safety factor associated with them. If they are performed correctly, they will not promote instability or impingement.

Exercise #1 –
Lying Reverse Flyes

The best movement for strengthening the external rotators is technically known as "prone abduction with external rotation." In the interest of simplicity I'm going to call them lying reverse flyes. Figure 4.2 shows the movement at the beginning and at the end of a repetition.

Start

Finish

Figure 4.2
Lying reverse flyes are best for strengthening the external rotators.
– Kelly Ryan

This exercise is best done lying face down on a bench. Resistance can be provided by using a dumbell or elastic tubing. To learn the movement, you may want to try it first without resistance. Do the following:
1. Lie face down on a bench with your arms hanging to the side.
2. Lift your arm out from your side like an airplane wing. In this position, your arm is at a 180-degree angle to your body.
3. Position your hand so your thumb is pointing up toward the ceiling.

Lenda Murray

4. To maximally stimulate the external rotators, reposition your arm slightly headward so it is now making an angle of approximately 100 degrees to your body.

5. Perform the movement with your arm in this position by lowering your arm toward the floor and then raising it toward the ceiling. Stop the movement at or just below shoulder height.

6. Concentrate on keeping your arm locked at the elbow and your thumb pointing up.

7. Do the movement slowly and pause for one or two seconds at the top.

You may do the movement one arm at a time or with both arms simultaneously. Also, most individuals should use minimal resistance when beginning this exercise. A two- or three-pound dumbell is usually sufficient. This exercise also strengthens the supraspinatus, and somewhat surprisingly, the subscapularis, the levator scapula, and the lats.

Exercise #2 –
30-degree Dumbell Raises

This exercise is very good for strengthening the supraspinatus, anterior and middle deltoids, subscapularis and the lower portion of the serratus anterior. It is technically referred to as "scaption with internal rotation." Commonly referred to as 30-degree dumbell raises. Figure 4.3 shows the correct form for the exercise. The movement can be performed standing or seated.

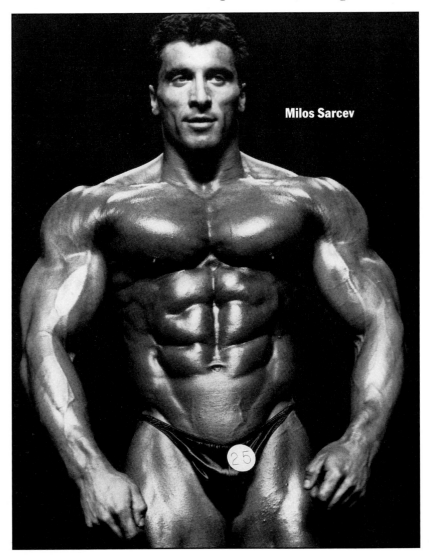

Milos Sarcev

Finish

Start

Figure 4.3
30-degree dumbell raises strengthen the supraspinatus and other shoulder muscles. Be sure your elbows stay below shoulder height. – Kelly Ryan

The arm is lifted away from the body while making an angle of approximately 30 degrees. To perform this exercise do the following:

1. Stand or sit with your arms by your side, holding a light dumbell or gripping elastic tubing anchored to the floor. (You may anchor the tubing by standing on it.)

2. Lift your arm, keeping it at an angle of 30 degrees to your body (90 degrees would be straight out in front as when performing front raises for the anterior deltoid and zero degrees would be out to the side as when performing lateral raises for the middle deltoid).

3. Concentrate on keeping your thumbs pointing down toward the floor and your elbows locked.

4. Stop the movement just below shoulder height, performing it slowly and pausing at the top.

Exercise #3 – Prone Dumbell Rows

This is similar to the movement that most individuals associate with building the lats and it may be inserted in your back routine. It is an excellent exercise for strengthening all three parts of the trapezius muscle, the rhomboids, the middle and rear deltoid and the levator scapula. Although shrugs are the most commonly performed exercise for strengthening the upper traps, prone rowing maximally stimulates the upper trapezius, according to the electromyograph data. These data indicate that shrugging movements actually stimulate the levator scapula more than the upper traps.

Marjo Selin

To ensure strict form, you should do this exercise lying face down on a high bench that allows a full stretch of the arm. To fully stimulate all three parts of the traps, the rhomboids, and the levator scapula, be sure you perform the movement keeping your back flat and avoid twisting the torso. Grasp a dumbell and let your arm stretch toward the floor. Keeping the elbow into your side, raise the dumbell toward your chest. Choose a dumbell that will allow you to perform the movement strictly, pausing at the top with the shoulder blades squeezed tightly together. Figure 4.4 shows the start and finish of the exercise.

Start

Finish

Figure 4.4
Prone dumbell rows
strengthen the
rhomboids, all three
parts of the traps and
the levator scapula.
– Kelly Ryan

Exercise #4 – Pressups

Pressups are the best exercise for strengthening the pec minor. The pressup also works the pec major and the lats. Perform the movement as follows:

1. Sit on a chair or bench. Depending on the ratio of your arm length to that of your torso it may be necessary to use handles of some sort, or dumbells will suffice (Figure 4.5).
2. Press down with your arms, lifting your body off the bench.

Figure 4.5
Pressups work the pec minor.
– Jeff Poulin

Exercise #5 – Pushups "With a Plus"

As mentioned previously, the serratus anterior is strengthened with 30-degree dumbell raises, although this exercise is not the best for providing maximal stimulation to the middle portion of the serratus. The best movement is called pushups "with a plus" and is shown in Figure 4.6. This exercise is similar to a regular pushup with the following modifications:

Start

Figure 4.6
Pushups "with a plus"
strengthen the serratus
anterior and the pec major.
– Jeff Poulin

Finish

- The hand position is slightly more narrow.
- Rather than using a flat-hand placement, the fist is used.
- Most importantly, at the top of the movement the shoulder blades are pulled forward as in a punching movement. This is the portion of the exercise that fully recruits the serratus anterior.

This exercise also works the pec major and minor and if you need to limit the number of exercises you are adding because of time constraints, you can insert this exercise into your chest routine, or you can also strengthen the serratus by making sure you include close-grip chinups, dumbell pullovers, and/or straight-arm pulldowns in your back routine.

What About Stretching?

We all know that flexibility is important and that flexibility is maintained by stretching. Unfortunately, we often adopt the philosophy, "if a little is good, a lot must be better." This is not necessarily true with respect to flexibility. In the case of the shoulder, excessive flexibility equates to instability.

Sue Price

That doesn't mean that stretching should be avoided. However, the type and amount of stretching recommended depends on whether you have pre-existing instability and what area of the shoulder is unstable. If instability is present, stretching should be done cautiously to avoid stretching those structures that are already lax. In severe cases of instability it may be better to avoid stretching and ask a sports therapist for suggestions.

Maintaining flexibility of the shoulder joint is important; it will enhance performance and may play a role in reducing the risk of shoulder injury. It has also been found that many individuals

A brief warm up period consisting of low-level cardiovascular exercise such as stationary cycling is recommended prior to stretching.
– Dr. Christine Lydon

Debbie Kruck

with unidirectional instability, say for instance, instability of only the anterior shoulder, will have a corresponding tightness of the posterior shoulder. These individuals will benefit from stretching the rear shoulder but should avoid aggressive stretching of the front portion of the shoulder.

Currently, there is some disagreement among experts regarding when, how often, how much and exactly how to stretch. Interestingly, it has been found that overstretching can actually cause muscles to become tighter because of a built-in reflex response that protects the muscle from being injured. Stretching is most effective when the soft tissues to be lengthened are warm. So a brief warmup period consisting of low-level cardiovascular exercise such as stationary cycling is recommended prior to stretching. You are sufficiently warm when you feel yourself just beginning to sweat.

The main structures that are usually included in a flexibility program for the shoulder are the anterior structures, including the pec major and the biceps, the posterior structures,

Maintaining flexibility of the shoulder joint is important; it will enhance performance and may play a role in reducing the risk of shoulder injury.

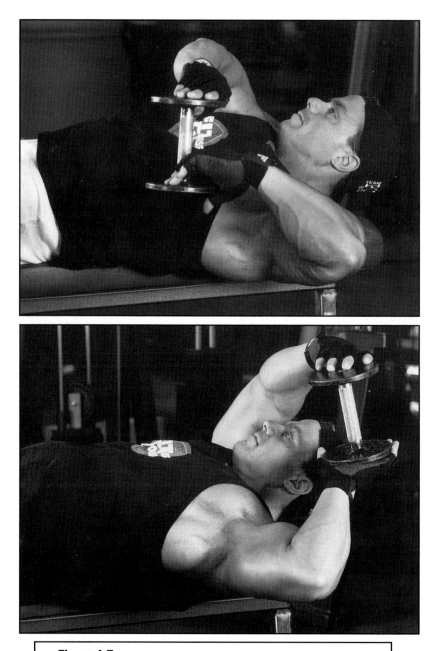

Figure 4.7
Stretching the external (top) and internal (bottom)
rotators of the shoulders. – Jeff Poulin

including the rear deltoids and posterior capsule, the internal and external rotators, the lats, and the triceps. Most experts agree that the safest and most effective approach to stretching is a technique that involves two phases. First, the structures are put in a slightly stretched position and held for a count of 20. From this stretched position, a slight resistance is given in the direction opposite the stretch for a count of ten. In other words, you lightly contract the muscles being stretched. This is followed by relaxation and a slow, cautious stretch into a new, slightly more stretched position. Illustrations showing stretches for the internal and external rotators are shown in Figure 4.7. You may use a small dumbell or similar object.

Gunter Schlierkamp

Sue Gafner

Conclusion

Following these suggestions will reduce your chances of suffering a shoulder injury and may improve an existing problem. But there is no substitute for professional advice and treatment rendered by a qualified physician. Beware of the personal trainer who believes he or she is qualified to evaluate and diagnose your problem, though, some personal trainers may be very qualified to carry out rehabilitative training once your problem has been diagnosed.

If you are experiencing shoulder pain or problems, it is usually recommended that you first seek conservative treatment which can be provided by a medical or chiropractic physician specializing in sports injuries. Sometimes conservative treatment is not always effective or appropriate and some type of surgical repair may be necessary, but conservative measures are usually attempted first. If conservative care is not appropriate, you will be referred to an orthopedic physician for further evaluation and treatment.

References

1) American Academy of Orthopedic Surgeons. *Athletic Training and Sports Injuries*, 1991.
2) Blackburn, T.A., et al. "EMG Analysis of Posterior Rotator Cuff Exercises." *Athletic Training.* 25:40 (1990).
3) Mosely, J.B. Jr., et al. "EMP Analysis of the Scapular Muscles during a Shoulder Rehabilitation Program." *American Journal of Sports Medicine.* 20:128 (1992).
4) Rowe, C.R., ed. *The Shoulder.* New York: Churchill Livingstone. n.d.
5) Souza, Thomas A. *Sports Injuries of the Shoulder, Conservative Management.* New York: Churchill Livingston, 1994.
6) Townsend, H., et al. "Electromyographic Analysis of the Glenohumeral Muscles during a Baseball Rehabilitation Program." *American Journal of Sports Medicine.* 19:264 (1991).

Alq́ Gurley

About the Author

Cynthia Humphreys, M.S., D.C., is a chiropractor specializing in the treatment, prevention and rehabilitation of sports injuries and other musculoskeletal condition. She is also a certified personal fitness trainer and massage therapist and has developed exercise therapy and rehabilitation programs for hundreds of patients. Dr. Humphreys specializes in and has great success treating and rehabilitating shoulder injuries. She also has a love for bodybuilding and weight training having pursued it as a means of staying fit and strong for over 15 years. She may be contacted at InLine Chiropractic, 21611 Stevens Creek Blvd., Cupertino, CA 95014, (408) 777-8182 or by e-mail at www.inlinechiro.com.

Acknowledgements

The author would like to express appreciation to Kelii and Mark Rifkin of World Gym, Campbell, CA and Joseph F. Scannell, D.C., Franco Germinario, D.D., and Sue Ellen Shima-Germinario, D.C. of Family Health Centre Chiropractic, San Leandro, CA for use of their facilities. And a special thanks to Thomas Souza, D.C., of Palmer College of Chiropractic-West for his contribution to my understanding of shoulder injuries.

Contributing Photographers

Jim Amentler, Garry Bartlett, Irvin Gelb, Robert Kennedy and Jason Mathas